TOPZ 10 HEROES OF THE BIBLE...

Hi! We're the Topz Gang!

Three cheers for you for picking up this book – because if stories are your thing, you are going to be bowled over by Benny and Paul's pick of their Topz 10 Bible heroes!

Did you know that the Bible is crammed with exciting tales of men and women who left their 'ordinary' selves far behind, and became heroes for God?

Through God's power:

- **Scared people can be brave**
- **Sad people can find the answers to their problems**
- **Unexpected people can change history**
- **Hurt people can learn to forgive**
- **Doubtful people can grow huge faith**
- **Worried people can start to trust**
- **Evil people can become good**
- **Unlikely people can become God's super-workers!**

You're about to discover 10 people with a sense of adventure and enough faith to live full-on for God. Wherever that took them and whatever it led them to do! What mattered was putting God first, living the way He wanted them to live, and doing what He asked them to do.

Following God like that isn't easy. It means trusting Him to help you in everything – and believing that He will never stop loving you.

Let the 10 heroes in this book fill you up with excitement and show you that life with God is

THE ABSOLUTE STONKING BEST!

Fill in and colour in the next page, then – happy reading!

1

SAMUEL
God's messenger

Read all about him in *1 SAMUEL 1 & 3*

Do you find it easy to do as you're told? At home and at school? We'd like to say we do, but honestly, a lot of the time, we just don't! Especially if it's something we *really* don't want to do… like tidying our bedrooms when we'd rather be playing in the park with the Gang. Or doing homework when all we actually want to do is NOTHING AT ALL!

When there's nothing going on, I get the fidgets. I can't just sit and do nothing. In fact, the only time I feel like doing nothing is when someone tells me I've got to do something I don't want to do…

See what we mean? Being obedient can be really hard.

What sort of things do you get told or asked to do that, most of the time, you really don't feel like? Write them down here.

_____

_____

_____

Now write down some things you'd rather be doing instead!

_____

_____

_____

There is one thing I *always* do when I'm told to: eat up everything on my plate!

There are two books in the Old Testament of the Bible called Samuel.

> **1 Samuel and 2 Samuel – nice and easy...**

And guess what? A very important man called Samuel appears in the first book of Samuel, but not in the second.

When we first read about Samuel, he's not even been born yet. His mum, Hannah, was sad all the time because she didn't have any children. So she asked God over and over to please give her a son.

Crack the code to read Hannah's prayer, and write it below.

A	B	C	D	E	F	G	H	I	J	K	L	M
N	O	P	Q	R	S	T	U	V	W	X	Y	Z

_____

_____

_____

_____

Answer in 1 Samuel 1 v 11.

9

God said, 'Yes' to Hannah and, **AT LONG LAST, SHE HAD A BABY.** A little boy she called – wait for it – Samuel! Stonking, hey? And Hannah would have thanked God a million times over!

But now she had a promise to keep. Hannah had promised to give Samuel back to God, only – how hard must it have been for her to do that?!

Still, Hannah didn't forget about it, or try to pretend it didn't matter. She didn't decide not to keep her promise after all, so that she could keep Samuel all for herself.

No. Hannah stayed faithful to God.

When Samuel was old enough (but still only a boy), she took him to a place called Shiloh where people went to worship God. She left him with Eli the priest, who would teach him and look after him. And from that moment on, Samuel's work for God began.

In fact, that's when **SAMUEL'S GREAT ADVENTURE WITH GOD BEGAN!**

Right from the start, God knew Samuel was going to be very special to Him. He knew that Samuel would listen to and obey Him.

God knew Samuel could be a hero for Him. So, God made him a prophet.

In other words, God chose Samuel to tell His people, the Israelites, what He wanted to say to them.

Wow! Being **GOD'S MESSENGER!** You don't get much more special than that, do you?

God knew that the very best person to be His messenger was Samuel.

But Samuel was just a young boy – a young boy who still had loads to learn about Him.

So did God…

- **Choose a grown-up who knew a lot to stand in for Samuel until he was older?**   YES ☐ NO ☐

- **Send Samuel off to prophet school to learn how to be a proper messenger?**   YES ☐ NO ☐

- **Change His mind about Samuel because, after all, he was still just a kid?**   YES ☐ NO ☐

- **Find someone well-known and respected instead?**   YES ☐ NO ☐

If you answered 'NO' to all of those questions, you're absolutely right!

GOD WASN'T AFTER SOMEONE WHO KNEW EVERYTHING.

He wasn't after someone other people thought was great. He wasn't even after all-grown-up Eli the priest, Samuel's teacher.

It was Samuel who was perfect for the job God wanted him to do. So, it was Samuel God chose.

Three times Samuel heard his name being called. Each time, he ran to Eli, who was also trying to sleep, saying, 'Here I am, Eli. You called me.'

The first two times Samuel woke him, Eli said, 'I didn't call you. Go back to bed.'

It wasn't until the third time it happened that Eli realised it was God who was calling Samuel.

Eli told Samuel to go back to bed. If Samuel heard the voice again, Eli told him to answer.

Colour in the dotted shapes to find out what Eli told Samuel to say.

Answer in 1 Samuel 3 v 9.

Woah! Just think about this – not only was God calling out to Samuel, but Eli was basically telling Samuel to say, 'Here I am, Lord. What do you want me to do?'

No matter how much we might want to serve God, actually saying, 'What do you want me to do?' can seem a little bit scary. It does to us. Does it to you?

Plenty of people in the Bible were scared when God asked them to do things too. They had to learn that if God wanted them to do something, He would give them everything they needed to do it.

God never leaves us to struggle on our own.

But, as you know, Samuel was just a young boy. *Really* young. **HE WAS JUST A KID.** He hadn't had time to learn a lot about God. Certainly not nearly as much as Eli.

So, how do you think he would have felt? Would he have pretended he didn't hear from God again? Would he have made up excuses as to why he couldn't answer God the way Eli told him to? Excuses like:

- **'I can't do that right now, Eli, I think I'm getting a cold.'**

- **'I won't offer to be God's servant today – I want to be free when Mum visits.'**

- **'Well, I would, Eli, but I've already got plans and it's sort of tricky to change them now.'**

The fact is that Samuel didn't say any of that. He didn't make excuses for not answering God. Not a single one!

Samuel hopped back into bed and when God called again – 'Samuel!' – he answered, 'Speak, Lord, your servant is listening,' just as Eli had told him to.

But that was just the start of Samuel's obedience. Now he'd told God he was ready to serve Him, he had to actually *be* ready.

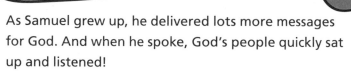

The very first message God gave to Samuel was bad news for Eli's family, who didn't obey God. Samuel didn't want to tell Eli what God had said, but Eli told him he must. So Samuel did.

As Samuel grew up, he delivered lots more messages for God. And when he spoke, God's people quickly sat up and listened!

God even gave Samuel the task of appointing the first two kings of Israel. You see? Samuel was asked to do some seriously important stuff!

The amazing thing about Samuel was that he didn't always want to obey God – but *HE OBEYED HIM ANYWAY.* What a hero!

Samuel was:

- **Brave enough to obey Eli**
- **Ready to deliver God's good messages and the bad ones too**
- **Obedient even if he didn't always agree with what God wanted him to do**
- **Prepared to be used by God in God's plans for His people**
- **Willing to grab hold of his adventure with God with both hands!**

Write your name in the speech bubble.

Now say your name out loud and imagine God is calling you. Are you ready to answer like our *HERO NUMBER 1, SAMUEL?* 'Speak, Lord, your servant is listening.'

If you are, pray this prayer...

God, thank You for hero Samuel, who teaches me so much about being brave and willing and obedient. Help me to listen out for You, God. Then, when I hear You, help me to be bold like Samuel, and ready to say, 'Yes, God!' I want to be all set for the adventures You have planned for me! Amen.

2 NOAH
God's great friend
Read all about him in *GENESIS 6–9*

Friendship is really important to God. But He doesn't just want us to be good friends to each other – He wants us to be friends with Him too! This next hero, our number 2, was an amazing friend to God.

You're almost certain to have heard of him. The story of Noah and his ark is probably one of the most famous stories in the whole of the Old Testament!

But how often do people read Noah's story and realise just what a hero he really was? When everyone around decided they didn't need God, Noah stuck with Him. When everyone around laughed at Noah for doing what God told him to do, he didn't give up. **HE DIDN'T FOLLOW THE CROWD.**

Hero Noah kept trusting God and kept following His instructions. If God told him to do something, Noah knew there was a very good reason for it.

Sometimes when I need God to help me trust Him, I ask for faith like Noah's.

How can we be faithful friends to God, the way Noah was?

Read through this list and tick the things you do:

Talk to God ☐

Read the Bible ☐

Listen to what God might be saying to you – as you talk to Him, through what you read in the Bible and what other Christians can teach you ☐

Obey God – know His guidelines for your life and follow them ☐

Ask God to forgive you for anything you may do wrong – so it doesn't get in the way of your friendship with Him ☐

Put other people first when you can ☐

Meet up with other Christians so you can encourage each other ☐

Tell others about God – that He loves them and wants to be part of their lives ☐

Trust Him totally to know what's best for you, and to do what's best for you ☐

Everything on the list is a brilliant way to show God you're serious about being friends with Him. If there's something you're not doing, why not make a start? Most of these are things you can do every day.

Noah trusted God because He knew Him well, and knew God loved him. And the more time we spend with God, the more we'll get to know Him too – the same as with all our other friends.

Have you got best mates you know really, *really* well? Let's find out! Think of three of them. Write down their names then, in the space below each one, write three things you know they like a lot, and three things they don't like at all.

Friend's name: _____

Likes: _____

Dislikes: _____

Friend's name: _____

Likes: _____

Dislikes: _____

Friend's name: _____

Likes: _____

Dislikes: _____

Next time you see these friends, ask them if you're right!

Noah lived close to God – all the time. We can do that too! **GOD CREATED US TO BE HIS FRIENDS.** What He wants is to share our lives – just like our friends on earth do.

That's what He wanted way back in Old Testament times as well. But, just like now, sadly a lot of people didn't want to know God – in fact, all of them! Except Noah. The Bible calls Noah: 'the only good man of his time' (Genesis 6 v 10). He was the only one who listened to God, stood up for God and loved God.

> Even though the Bible calls Noah 'the only good man', God included Noah's family in His plans too. Noah had a wife and three married sons.

Crack the code to see what the sons were called.

A	B	C	D	E	F	G	H	I	J	K	L	M
∧	□	◉	▷	▽	▶	⊙	▷	▣	□	◁	⊠	△

N	O	P	Q	R	S	T	U	V	W	X	Y	Z
⊠	▽	▷	▷	◁	◁	⊕	⊡	◁	⊞	⊟	⊕	◁

_____

_____

Answer on page 110.

God had created a perfect world, but the people He'd made to live there and be His friends had spoilt it. So, because they were selfish and greedy and didn't care about Him, God decided to start all over again.

God would send heavy rain to fall on the earth day after day after day. In fact, the rain would last for 40 days and 40 nights, and no one would be saved from the huge flood.

Except Noah and his family.

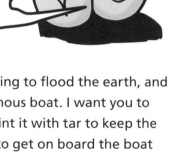

And, of course, rather a lot of animals!

So God said to Noah, 'I'm going to flood the earth, and I want you to build an enormous boat. I want you to make rooms inside it and paint it with tar to keep the water out. Then I want you to get on board the boat with your wife, your sons and their wives. Oh, yes, and I also want you to load up two of every kind of animal and bird so that they'll be safe with you…'

AND NOAH DID EVERYTHING, EXACTLY THE WAY GOD TOLD HIM TO.

When other people saw Noah building a boat, they thought he was really bonkers! They probably already thought he was odd because he obeyed God when no one else bothered. But the boat thing? Madness!

Noah's feelings may have been hurt by what other people thought and by what they said. After all, no one likes to be laughed at. But the most important thing to Noah was God. He trusted God and he would obey Him – no matter what.

Here's a list of some of the animals and birds that might have ended up with Noah on the boat. Can you find them all in the word search?

```
D Z A Z D Y E K F B G M B D
R E L E P H A N T M D E J O
G A E T C X A L W V H E I N
T G M B O I Q U A I L S U K
E L M A N R D F L K I O S E
P E A B H O R S E U U R T Y
I G Y K I N N A N E J E Q G
P R A B B I T M P Q K C Q H
E T E A T U G O P L D O E F
E X U H Y O L K M E I N P Q
H J S W S E O N N T N I D R
S U M A T O P O P P I H C S
A E L N I M A R Y O W R O B
T D A K S E S U O M W Y E A
```

Answer on page 110.

PARROT   **MOUSE**

SHEEP   **EAGLE**

DONKEY   **HIPPOPOTAMUS**

ELEPHANT   **QUAIL**

RABBIT   **ANTELOPE**

RHINOCEROS   **HORSE**

How do you feel when someone teases you? Or, worse, bullies you? If I hear that people have been talking about me behind my back, I just want to hide in my bedroom with Saucy and never come out...

Have any of those things ever happened to you? How did you feel?

_____

_____

_____

_____

However Noah felt, he had hero strength inside him. God had given him a massive job to do. This was a BIG boat he had to build and there were a LOT of animals to find. And Noah did it.

Not only that, but he pretty much did it all by himself! Just imagine that for a minute... You see, Noah didn't have a huge team. No one else wanted to know God, so Noah only had his family to help him. And still he did exactly as God asked him to.

NOAH TRUSTED GOD IN A FANTASTIC HERO WAY – because he had to trust Him just about all on his own.

And the trust didn't end once everyone was safely on board the boat.

When rain pours down and it's really heavy, it can be quite scary. It can be really loud, and there might be thunder and lightning. You've probably seen pictures of bad floods too, or maybe you've been affected by flooding, or know people who have.

Imagine Noah and his family – stuck on a boat in a rainstorm that lasted for 40 days and nights! Imagine the water coming up and up and up with no sign of it stopping!

Would the boat be strong enough and waterproof enough? Would the food they'd brought with them last long enough? Would the rain ever stop? Would they ever see dry land again…?

But through every last raindrop, Noah held on to God. He believed God would keep His promise, and make sure they were all safe.

This was tough, but Noah trusted God enough to stay His very good friend.

He trusted God enough to know that God would keep being *his* very good friend too.

Super-cool hero!

When we've got problems or worries and they're making us miserable, it can feel a bit as though we're stuck in a flood. We want to feel happy and safe again, but there seems to be so much to sort out and do before we can.

If ever you feel like that, try to remember these three things:

1. **God wants you to talk to Him about your worries.**

2. **You can trust God to help you sort things out.**

3. **God kept Noah safe through the flood, and He will stay close to you and keep you safe too.**

The rain did stop for Noah. Little by little, the water did go down.

One day, when Noah sent out a dove from the boat to see what it would find, it flew back to him with a leafy twig from an olive tree in its beak. That's how Noah knew the land was starting to appear again.

How excited he must have been! God had kept His promise and saved him and his whole family.

NOAH, our **HERO NUMBER 2,** was a hero of a friend to God. He stood up for God and was faithful, even when it might have seemed easier just to go along with everyone else and forget about Him. God longs for us to be His friends. He longs for us to trust Him – through good times and through tricky times.

Why not ask God to help you be a hero of a friend to Him, like Noah?

God, when I have problems and worries and life seems difficult, teach me to hold on to You. Help me to stick with You, even if people around me don't want to know You. Please give me hero faith like Noah to obey You and to follow You. Thank You for being my friend, forever and ever. I love You. Amen.

3 ANNA
A powerhouse for God
Read all about her in *LUKE 2*

On a scale of 1 to 10, where would you rate your patience?

I don't know about you, but I have good days and bad days. On a good day, when everything's cool, I find it quite easy to be patient.

Paul's patience scale (good day)

1 2 3 4 5 6 7 8 9 10

On a bad day, I can get grumpy. And when I'm grumpy, it's tough to be patient about anything.

Paul's patience scale (bad day)

1 2 3 4 5 6 7 8 9 10

Why not rate your own patience for good days and bad days? Draw in your arrows on the patience scales.

One of the things that makes me grumpy is when Mum says I can't go out until I've done my homework! What sort of things make you grumpy and impatient? Make a list here.

_____

_____

_____

_____

_____

_____

_____

_____

_____

Wow! Let's just hope all of that doesn't happen on the same day!

God wants us to try to be patient, no matter what's going on or how we feel. Even if we've had the worst day ever! And it's not easy. That's why, when we give our lives to God, He sends His Holy Spirit to live inside us to help us.

With God's Spirit inside us, we can learn to be all sorts of things that are much, MUCH harder to be without Him.

> In fact, when we have the Holy Spirit inside us and we keep close to God every day, there are quite a few things other people may start to see in us.

Want to know what they are? Here's a list (which you can find in the Bible in Galatians 5 v 22–23), but all the words are back to front. Write them out the correct way round and say them out loud.

evoL   _____

yoJ   _____

ecaeP   _____

ecneitaP   _____

ssendniK   _____

ssendooG   _____

ssenlufhtiaF _____

ytilimuH   _____

lortnoc-fleS _____

Answers on page 110.

Hero number 3 in our Topz 10 was full to the brim with everything on the list!

Anna may only be mentioned in three short verses in the New Testament but, boy, is she a hero for God!

She was bursting with energy for Him – which is quite something, because she was 84 years old!

Follow the read-around to see how Anna spent her time.

START

'SHE NEVER LEFT THE TEMPLE; DAY AND NIGHT SHE WORSHIPPED GOD, FASTING AND PRAYING.'

(Luke 2 v 37)

Serving God was Anna's whole life. She was a prophet, so she did as God wanted her to do and spoke the words God wanted her to say.

The Bible tells us that Anna was only married for seven years. So, as she was now 84 she had probably been a widow for a long time.

AND WHAT HAD SHE DONE WITH ALL THAT TIME?

She gave it to God!

Imagine waking up any day of the week – tomorrow, say – knowing you could do exactly what you wanted.

What would you do? How would you spend the time?

Write down everything you can think of here.

_____

_____

_____

_____

_____

_____

_____

The thing about Anna is that **SERVING GOD WAS HOW SHE WANTED TO SPEND HER TIME.**
It wasn't hard for her – it was as natural as eating! She wanted to totally devote herself to Him.

But devoting herself to God didn't mean ignoring people. It didn't mean Anna thought, 'I'm glad I'm friends with God, and I don't really care about anyone else!'

It meant sharing God's love with as many people as possible, and telling them what God wanted them to know. It meant being God's servant – and obeying Him.

Now make another list; only this time, think about how God would like you to spend your time.

God loves you, so what could you do to show God you love Him? How could you show God's love to other people?

Anna's story starts with patience.

It's so easy to lose patience – especially when you're just itching for something to happen.

So, imagine having to wait for something for years and years and years... and YEARS!

Well, on top of being all-out for God, **ANNA HAD HERO PATIENCE.**

Over hundreds of years, prophets had been telling God's people that God would send someone special to them. A King. A Saviour – Jesus. This was God's promise. But they weren't told *when* this Saviour would come – simply that He *would*.

So that's what God's people had to believe. That's what they had to hold on to. Even if it meant waiting for what seemed like forever.

> And believe me, it was a long wait. A long, long, LONG wait. And, for Anna, almost her whole life had passed (she was 84, remember) – and she was still waiting!

But Anna waited with rock-solid faith. She just knew that, one day, this special person would arrive on the earth. There were no 'if's or 'maybe's for Anna: God had promised. That meant it would happen.

ANNA NEVER GAVE UP. She never lost heart. And through all those years of waiting, she encouraged others to wait and to believe in God's promise too.

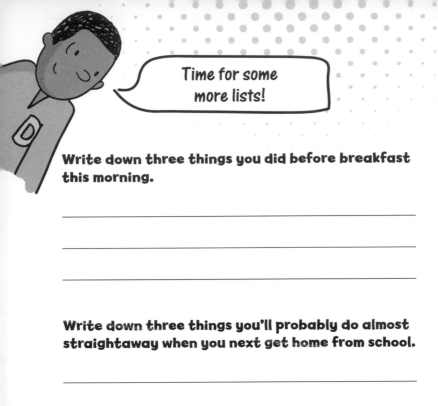

Time for some more lists!

Write down three things you did before breakfast this morning.

_____

_____

_____

Write down three things you'll probably do almost straightaway when you next get home from school.

_____

_____

_____

Did you know that God sees all those things? He sees the things you've already done and the things you've still to do.

Anna waited on God, and worked for God. But she didn't do that because she wanted God to see what a 'good' person she was, and then reward her. Anna did everything she did because she loved God with her whole heart.

Of course, God _did_ see the way Anna lived her life – because God sees everything. And God _did_ reward her.

As a prophet, Anna told other people what God wanted them to know. She was also very wise and she saw things other people couldn't see.

When Jesus was a baby, His parents took Him to the Temple in Jerusalem to present Him to God, as was the custom. Well – as soon as Anna saw the baby Jesus, she knew instantly who He was. God showed her that He was the Saviour His people had been waiting for – for SUCH a long time.

This was Anna's reward!

Not only did she know for certain that the Saviour had arrived at last – **SHE ALSO GOT TO MEET HIM FACE-TO-FACE!** And she quite probably gave Him a cuddle too!

God knew how devoted Anna was to Him. So He gave her the chance to welcome Jesus to the earth. He's such a cool Father God!

So, what did Anna do next? Crack the code to find out.

A	B	C	D	E	F	G	H	I	J	K	L	M
◭	◖	◉	▷	▽	▶	◉	▶	□	◁	◨	⊟	◭

N	O	P	Q	R	S	T	U	V	W	X	Y	Z
⊠	▽	▷	▷	◁	◀	⊕	◉	◁	⊞	⊖	⊞	◁

Anna...

'◉◭◁▽ ⊕▷◭⊠⊠◁ ⊕▽ ◉▽▷ ◭⊠▷

◁▷▽⊠▽ ◭◭▽◉⊕ ⊕▷◭ ◉▷□⊞▷ ⊕▽

◭⊟⊟ □▷▽ □▽◁◭ □◭□⊕□⊠◉ ▷▽◁

◉▽▷ ⊕▽ ◁▽⊕ ◁▽◁▷◁◭⊟▽◭ ▷◁▽▽.'

_____

_____

_____

_____

Answer in Luke 2 v 38.

You see? A total powerhouse for God!

Nothing could ever stop **ANNA,** our **HERO NUMBER 3,** from living her life all out for Him – even at 84 years old! Why not say this prayer now?

God, I want to be a powerhouse for You. When I talk to You, please help me to have hero patience and to know that I must wait for You to answer – even if I have to wait for a long time. Teach me never to give up on Your promises. And if there's a chance to tell someone else about You, make me brave enough! Amen.

4

STEPHEN
Filled with God's Spirit
Read all about him in *ACTS 6–7*

Time for a top 10: the top 10 most important things in the whole wide world to you and to me!

I'll go first – here's my list of 10 things that mean the most to me right at this very moment:

1. My family

2. Telling jokes and making people laugh

3. The Gang and being part of it

4. Talking to God

5. Riding my bike

6. Having God's Son, Jesus, as my friend

7. Bacon sandwiches!

8. Waking up on Saturday mornings with NO SCHOOL!

9. Summer camping holidays

10. Going out for ice cream after church

The trouble is, there are SO many people I care about

and SO many things I like doing (and eating), it's actually quite hard to stick to just 10!

Write your top 10 list of stonking things that mean the most to you (if 10 isn't enough, there are a few extra lines at the end for you to write more).

1. _____
2. _____
3. _____
4. _____
5. _____
6. _____
7. _____
8. _____
9. _____
10. _____
_____
_____
_____

When someone or something means a lot to you, you want to talk about it, don't you? You want to tell someone what you've done with your best friend, or where you've been on your holiday.

You might want to say why you love something so much, or what's so special about the people who are important to you.

I went on a cycling-camping holiday with my auntie and uncle and my cousin, Josh. It was the best holiday in the world! We cycled around with all our gear strapped to our bikes. It didn't rain once. I loved it SO much, I must have talked about it to the Gang for weeks afterwards. Weeks and weeks!

Months actually. Months and months...

It's hard to keep quiet about the things that matter. If you're excited about something, you just want to talk about it...

But somehow, **EVEN THOUGH YOU LOVE GOD, IT CAN BE VERY TRICKY TO TALK ABOUT HIM.**

It's easy to talk about God with those who also know and love Him. The hard part can come when someone who doesn't know God suddenly asks you about Him. Or there's a chance to stand up for God – or a moment to tell someone you're a Christian, who doesn't know that about you.

And if you don't know God but want to find out more about Him, starting to ask questions can be hard as well.

If you're the only Christian in your family or in your class at school, it can be tough. Sometimes, people can make fun of others who live life with God. And in some places in the world, it's actually dangerous to be a Christian (as it was for our next hero).

You can find the story of our hero number 4 in the book of Acts in the New Testament.

After Jesus died and went back to heaven, God sent His Holy Spirit to the earth. The Spirit came to live inside people who love God, to help them:

- **Live God's way**

- **Talk to God**

- **Remember all the things Jesus taught**

- **Be brave enough to tell others how much God loves them and wants to forgive them – so that one day they can live with Him forever**

One man who was filled to the absolute brim with the Holy Spirit was Stephen. Write out the following words the right way round to find out what the Bible calls him.

'a nam ylhcir desselb yb doG dna lluf fo rewop'

_____

_____

_____

Answer in Acts 6 v 8.

41

Stephen was picked to join a team who would help look after poor widows in Jerusalem.

As well as that, he went out and about, teaching people about Jesus.

Before Jesus went back to heaven, He told His friends to tell as many people as they could about Him:

'Go, then, to all peoples everywhere and make them my disciples' (Matthew 28 v 19).

Jesus wanted the whole world to know that He'd died to bring people back to God. To take away all the wrong things people do – the things that spoil their friendship with God.

Because Jesus came back to life, all anyone had to do to live with God in heaven forever was say sorry – really *be* sorry – and believe in Him. And Jesus wanted everyone to know that too.

Who *wouldn't* want to know that?! It's the best news ever!

The Bible doesn't tell us everything we might want to know about heaven, where we can go to be with God. But it does say this (sort out the scrambled words).

'There will be no more aehdt _____ , no more fireg _____ or ngryci _____ or apni _____. The old things have papsiadreed _____.'

Answer in Revelation 21 v 4.

Just imagine... In heaven, there will be:

- **Happiness, not sadness**
- **Peace, not fighting**
- **Good health, not illness**
- **Love, not hate**

But Jesus had enemies when He lived on the earth, and He had enemies now He lived in heaven.

So did the people who told others about Him – including Stephen.

Stephen knew God's Word inside out and back to front.

And because of the Holy Spirit inside him, **WHEN HE SPOKE, PEOPLE LISTENED.** When he taught them about God, no one could argue with what he said – not even his enemies!

This made it really hard for those who hated Stephen, and what he taught, to find a way to stop him. But Stephen did good and kind things for people and he only ever spoke the truth. How could they turn people against a man like that?

In the end, the only way Stephen's enemies could find anything bad to say about him was to tell lies.

You see, Stephen and the Holy Spirit together were...
(Put the letters in the correct number order.)

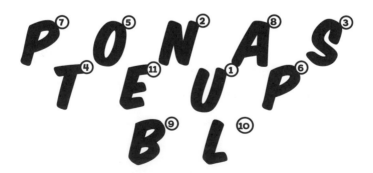

Stephen stood up for God with **_HERO STRENGTH AND BOLDNESS._**

He wasn't scared to tell important church leaders that they weren't obeying God properly.

He wasn't afraid to keep talking no matter how much they wanted him to stop.

God meant more to Stephen than anything, and he wouldn't keep quiet about Him.

God has done incredible things for us:

- **He has given us an awesome planet as our home.**

- **He has given us each other as our friends and family.**

- **He has given us Jesus as a way to mend our broken friendship with Him.**

On top of that, He loves us every day. And no matter what we say, or what we do, He will always love us and forgive us when we tell Him we're sorry.

No wonder Stephen wanted the world to know about Jesus!

Stephen was the first Christian to die for standing up for what he believed in.

There's a special word for someone who dies for their beliefs. Crack the Topz code to see what it is.

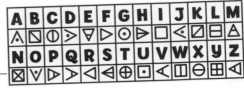

A	B	C	D	E	F	G	H	I	J	K	L	M
△	◹	◐	▷	▽	▶	⊙	▷	□	◁	⊘	⊟	△

N	O	P	Q	R	S	T	U	V	W	X	Y	Z
⊠	▽	▽	▷	▷	◁	◁	⊕	⊡	◁	▥	⊖	◁

The Holy Spirit gives people the power to do amazing things for God.

STEPHEN, our **HERO NUMBER 4,** shone with hero strength. Even his enemies could see it. When they looked at him, they saw that 'his face looked like the face of an angel' (Acts 6 v 15).

The Bible doesn't tell us what Stephen was like before the Holy Spirit came to live inside him. But afterwards, nothing could stop him from serving God like a hero. Nothing at all. Why not talk to God now?

Lord Jesus, help me to be a hero like Stephen, and to speak out for You. Please fill me with Your Holy Spirit so that I can feel strong enough to tell people about all the amazing things You've done. Help me not to be discouraged if people don't like me because I'm a Christian. You are worth it. Amen.

5

JOSEPH
From dreamer to leader

Read all about him in
GENESIS 37, 39–45

Have you ever been jealous of one of your brothers or sisters, or maybe one of your friends or someone at school?

Well, there's a lot of jealousy in the story of our hero number 5 too. Joseph had 11 brothers and almost all of them were jealous of him!

I get jealous of Sarah sometimes if we've had an argument about something, and it's me who gets in trouble from Mum. Even if it was my fault, it still feels as if Sarah's the favourite.

There are plenty of other reasons for feeling jealous too. Maybe someone in your class is always getting better marks than you. Or they always score more footie goals than you do.

And sometimes you can even *imagine* things about someone else and be jealous when they're not even true – a bit like John imagining Sarah is his mum's favourite twin!

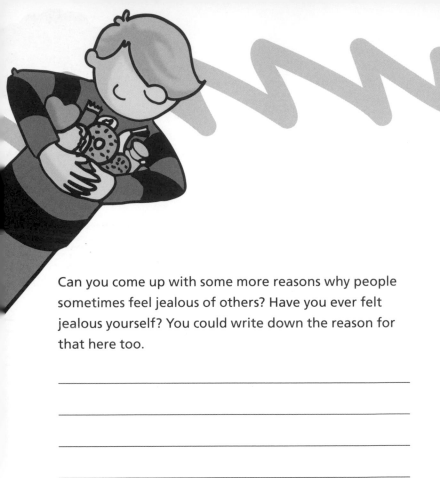

Can you come up with some more reasons why people sometimes feel jealous of others? Have you ever felt jealous yourself? You could write down the reason for that here too.

_____

_____

_____

_____

The big problem with feeling jealous is that, once you start, it's really hard to stop. And it makes you feel horrible. You can feel that you're not good enough. You might get angry with the person who's making you jealous. And when you feel angry enough with someone, you can even start to hate them.

Being wound up with all those feelings can make talking to God tricky too. So it's better to try to stop jealousy before it starts.

Want to know a really cool way to help yourself *not* to feel jealous of someone else? Don't look at what someone else has got that you haven't – or the way someone else is that you just aren't. Think about everything you've got to be thankful for instead.

> **The more you realise how much you can thank God for, the more you'll be able to enjoy those things – and the less time you'll spend being jealous of other people!**

Have a think right now, and here's a challenge: see if you can come up with your top 10 things you are grateful for, and write them all down here:

1. _____
2. _____
3. _____
4. _____
5. _____
6. _____
7. _____
8. _____
9. _____
10. _____

The main reason why hero Joseph's brothers were so jealous of him was because he really *was* their dad's (Jacob's) favourite. They weren't imagining it. Jacob was quite old when Joseph was born and he loved this son more than the others. He couldn't seem to help it.

The trouble was, by showing that Joseph was his favourite, Jacob made things worse for him.

And Joseph didn't help himself either. He didn't keep quiet about anything.

Jacob made an amazing coat for Joseph, and Joseph made sure his brothers knew about it.

Colour in Joseph's coat as brightly as you can!

But how do you think all this special treatment made Joseph's brothers feel?

Write out the back-to-front words the correct way round to find out.

'yeht detah rieht rehtorb'

Answer in Genesis 37 v 4.

Joseph had some strange dreams. It looked as though one day his whole family would bow down and worship him. Again, Joseph let his brothers know. And how did they feel?

'yeht detah mih neve erom'

Answer in Genesis 37 v 8.

Joseph's brothers probably thought he was being quite boastful. They might have said to each other, 'Does Joseph think he's better than we are?'

In case you're ever in danger of boasting about something you can do or something you have, turn the page for a Topz tip on how to stop yourself!

God has made us everything we are, and He's given us everything we have. If we're good at something, it's because God made us good at it and we should say thank You to Him. If we're lucky enough to have great stuff, then we should thank God for that too.

Do you get it? If you know – *really know* – that everything good comes from God, then you'll learn to thank Him for it – not boast about it. Great tip, hey!

Like jealousy, boasting can lead to people not liking each other – and Joseph's brothers really didn't like all the extra attention Joseph got.

In the end, they hated him so much that they wanted to kill him.

They decided they wouldn't actually kill him – but they still did something terrible. **THEY SOLD JOSEPH AS A SLAVE.** He was taken away from his home and his family to Egypt.

Then the brothers lied and told their dad, Jacob, that his favourite son had been killed by a wild animal.

What a pickle Joseph was in! And you're probably wondering, 'When does the hero bit start?'

Well, that would be right now!

Through every bad thing that happened to him, **JOSEPH DIDN'T BEHAVE BADLY.**

He could have done. He could have been a lazy slave. Or a grumpy slave. He could have blamed God for not getting him out of the mess he was now in.

But Joseph chose to stay faithful to God and to be good for Him. He worked hard for his new master and things turned out a lot better than they might have done. That was because… (Write out the words below in the correct number order.)

_____

_____

_____

_____

Answer in Genesis 39 v 2.

SUCCESSFUL⁹ JOSEPH⁵ HIM⁸ AND⁶ THE¹ WAS³ MADE⁷ WITH⁴ LORD²

Even then, things didn't seem to go to plan. Poor Joseph didn't do anything wrong, but **HE STILL ENDED UP IN PRISON.**

Again, though, he behaved very well!

He didn't cause trouble. He kept trusting God who 'was with Joseph and blessed him' (Genesis 39 v 21).

God blessed him *so* much that Joseph was actually put in charge of all the other prisoners!

What Joseph had was **HERO STICKABILITY!** He was stuck to God and no one and nothing could pull him away!

That's what makes Joseph so… (Trace over these letters and shout the word out loud!)

AWESOME!

Now with everything that had happened, it might have looked like God didn't have a plan – but He definitely did! And it was because Joseph loved God and trusted Him so much that God was able to use him in His plan.

God had given Joseph a gift. An amazing gift! Joseph was able to tell people **WHAT THEIR DREAMS MEANT.**

Now, the king of Egypt had been having some odd dreams. When he heard about Joseph's gift, he had him brought to him from prison.

The king asked Joseph what his dreams meant and Joseph told him: the next seven years would be good for Egypt. Lots of food would grow with plenty for everyone to eat.

'But,' Joseph said, 'the seven years after that will be bad. There won't be much food at all, so you must store up food during the good years so that you can feed people through the bad ones.'

The king knew straightaway that God had made Joseph wise. And guess what he did? He believed in Joseph enough to put him in charge of the whole of Egypt! One of Joseph's jobs would be to look after all the food.

I wish I could have that job!

Everything happened the way Joseph said it would. And in the seven bad years, it wasn't just Egypt that was short of food. There were hungry people everywhere. So they came to visit Joseph and he was able to feed them.

One day, a group of men turned up together. Follow the arrows from letter to letter to read who they were.

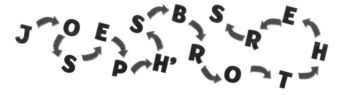

They didn't recognise Joseph, but he knew who they were. Uh-oh... Would he punish them for what they'd put him through?

No! Joseph forgave them – with **HERO FORGIVENESS!** God's plan was for Joseph to be in charge of Egypt so that he could save starving people. Because his family were hungry too, now God had brought Joseph's brothers back to him.

So that's **JOSEPH,** our **HERO NUMBER 5!** Why not talk to God now?

> *Thank You, God, for Joseph's hero stickability and forgiveness. When things are tough, help me to remember how Joseph stayed faithful and kept trusting You. Please teach me how to use my gifts for You, and not to boast about the things I'm good at or the things I have. Amen.*

6 MIRIAM
The girl with a hero heart
Read all about her in *EXODUS 1–2*

Does Sarah like having a twin brother?

I love it – most of the time! John's funny. If I'm feeling a bit down in the dumps, he can make me smile. Then there are other times when I don't like having a brother at all.

When Mum hears us arguing, we BOTH get in trouble – which is really unfair because he usually starts it! But mostly it's cool. And being twins feels sort of special.

Yep. If I had to pick someone to be my twin sister, I'd pick Sarah.

How about you? Do you have any brothers or sisters?

YES ☐   **NO** ☐

If **YES**:

How many brothers do you have?

_____

How many sisters do you have?

_____

If **NO**:

Would you like a brother or a sister?

YES ☐   **NO** ☐

Would you like them to be older or younger than you are?

_____

If you have brothers or sisters, what sort of things do you get up to together? Or if it's just you, what fun things can you do at home by yourself?

_____

_____

_____

_____

_____

Our hero number 6, Miriam, had a baby brother – and she was a real **HERO SISTER** to him. Even though she wasn't very old herself, when something terrible happened, she showed just how important her family was to her.

Miriam and her family lived in Egypt. They were Israelites – God's special people. A lot of Israelite people were living in Egypt then.

Now the Israelites weren't doing anything wrong, but there was a problem. The king of Egypt thought there were too many Israelites in his country. It made him nervous. He was worried that, one day, there would be SO many, they might try to take over.

Well, the king had a think. And what he thought was, 'If there weren't all these Israelite baby boys – there wouldn't be nearly so many new Israelites.'

So he did something.

Something horribly cruel.

Something terribly shocking.

He ordered that all the Israelite baby boys should be drowned in the River Nile.

Imagine how sad and scared God's people must have felt when they heard the king's order!

> More than sad. Heartbroken! God's heart must have been broken too.

Miriam's mum had just had a baby boy. Draw Miriam's face when her family found out what the king had ordered.

But Miriam's mum was having none of it. Miriam's mum put her foot down.

'No one is going to drown *my* baby!' she said. 'Not even the king.'

And she made a plan: she and the family would hide the baby boy away. Which they did – for three whole months.

Draw Miriam's face when she knew her mum wasn't going to give up her little brother.

Do you know much about babies? Let's see how easy they are to hide...

Look at this list and put a tick against the things that are true about babies, and a cross against the things that are false:

1. Babies sleep all the time ☐

2. Babies keep very still ☐

3. Babies never cry ☐

4. Babies need lots of attention ☐

5. Babies can make a huge noise ☐

6. Babies don't like cuddles ☐

7. Babies create lots of dirty laundry ☐

Answers on page 110.

Hiding a baby wouldn't have been easy! Miriam's family were trying to keep secret something that wriggled, could be VERY noisy, made a mess, probably didn't always smell too good(!), and wasn't going to be ignored! What a challenge!

But Miriam and her family were ready to do whatever they had to, to keep their little baby boy safe.

Only, what they *couldn't* do was stop him growing bigger. After three months, they realised – they couldn't keep him safe in their home forever.

So, **THEY HAD TO MAKE A NEW PLAN.**

Do you remember that the River Nile was mentioned at the start of this story? Well, it's just about to appear again, and play a very important part in what happened to Miriam's brother next.

DID YOU KNOW...?

- **The River Nile is thought to be the longest river in the whole, entire world (with the Amazon coming in a very close second!).**

- **It runs for about 6,695 kilometres (that's 4,160 miles).**

- **Lots of Egyptian people lived near the River Nile to be close to water and catch fish to eat.**

- **Because it was so long, the river was a good way for the Egyptian people to get from place to place – they could travel by boat.**

- **The land around the river was very good for growing crops – another good reason to live nearby.**

- **The Nile is a freshwater river, but it runs into the salty Mediterranean Sea.**

And do you know where the Nile got its name from? It comes from a Greek word that means 'river valley'. Colour in the dotted shapes to find out what it is.

So – why was the River Nile so important to Miriam and her family?

Well, it was about to become Miriam's baby brother's... (Unjumble the letters.)

dgiinh cepal

Answer on page 110.

Now, we know what you're thinking – how can you hide a baby in a river? Sounds like that could go REALLY WRONG! But Miriam's mum was very clever! She knew exactly what to do.

She took a basket and painted it all over with tar. This would make it waterproof. Next, she carefully tucked the little baby up inside. Then, she and Miriam went down to the river.

Some tall reeds grew out of the water close to the bank. That's where Miriam and her mum hid the basket. They slid it in among the reed stalks.

Miriam and her mum must have been so worried and upset! How could they leave this tiny baby all alone? How could they believe he'd be safe? Their hearts must have been broken all over again.

As Miriam's mum headed for home, Miriam stayed behind, a little way from the riverside. She wanted to keep an eye on the basket. She needed to know what would happen to the bundle inside.

Someone was on her way down to the river to bathe. Someone was about to spot the baby in the basket.

Who?

THE PRINCESS – the daughter of the king of Egypt himself! Miriam could have run away. She could have thought, 'I'd better sneak off. I might get in big trouble.' She could have felt she'd already done everything she could do.

But she didn't.

Miriam cared more for the safety of her little brother than for her own. She was only about seven years old herself, but **SHE UNDERSTOOD THAT LOVING SOMEONE MEANT PUTTING THEM FIRST.**

This hero sister would protect her little brother for as long as she could.

The princess found the basket. She saw the baby, crying inside. She knew he was one of the Israelite babies, but never in a million years could she hurt him.

And Miriam didn't hesitate. She went straight over to the princess and asked, 'Shall I find an Israelite woman to take care of this baby for you?'

The princess didn't hesitate either: 'Yes,' she said.

> Not only was Miriam just a kid, walking up to a princess – she was also an Israelite, marching up to a powerful Egyptian! Oodles of hero quality! Oodles of quick thinking too!

Oodles and oodles! Because, listen to this: Miriam ran to fetch, not just any old Israelite woman – but her and the baby's mum!

Miriam's mum had done her best, but she probably never thought she'd hold her baby ever again.

Until Miriam, through her boldness and quick thinking, caused a miracle!

The princess said to Miriam's mum: 'Take this baby and nurse him for me, and I will pay you' (Exodus 2 v 9).

So the baby was able to stay with his own family, in his own home, with his own mum and sister looking after him.

What a happy ending!

When he was older, the princess adopted the boy. She called him Moses. And Moses would grow up to become a great leader and prophet for God.

You see, God is amazing. In the middle of the terrible thing the king of Egypt did, **GOD STILL HAD A PLAN.** A plan to save baby Moses. And through our **HERO NUMBER 6, MIRIAM,** and her hero heart, God put it into action. Why not pray this prayer now?

> *God, however young I am, however old I am, I want to serve You. I want a hero heart like Miriam's. Please teach me to put other people first. Please show me ways I can look after my family and be a friend to others too. Please use me in Your plans, God. Amen.*

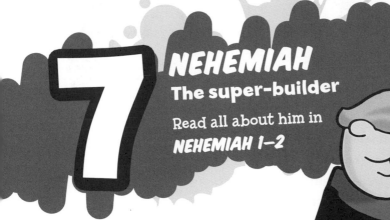

7 NEHEMIAH
The super-builder
Read all about him in
NEHEMIAH 1–2

Are you the sort of person who has hobbies? Some people do a few different things, don't they?

They might enjoy playing football, like Danny, and going cycling too, like Dave. Or they might want to spend time playing on the computer, like Paul – or trying lots of different food, like me!

Sometimes the hobbies people do are to do with things they're good at.

A hobby might also be something you want to get better at. Look at me – I do like playing the violin but I find it quite hard. If I keep practising, I'm hoping it'll get easier.

I've got loads of hobbies. I'm always finding new ones. I just love learning to do new things! Here's a list of my top 10!

1. **Playing on my computer** (I like to pretend I'm a spy and doing something top secret!)

2. **Zooming in my go-kart at the park** (I can go round bends really fast now)

3. **Finding out stuff** (one day I'd like to win a TV general knowledge quiz)

4. **Playing football** (I don't usually win, but who cares?!)

5. **Baking** (with Benny because we always make chocolate muffins!)

6. **Reading** (I love a good book – I always imagine the main character wears glasses)

7. **Ice skating** (I fall down a lot but it's soooo much fun!)

8. **Gardening** (a bit – I enjoyed it in the Gang when we grew sunflowers)

9. **Designing space rockets** (new hobby, but I've done four now – I reckon I'll make it to the moon one day)

10. **Taking Gruff for a walk with John** (I'd love a dog, but Dad doesn't want one messing up the lawn and Mum doesn't want one messing up the carpets... sigh...)

It's your turn to write your top 10! What hobbies do you like to do in your spare time? Or what would you like to do if you could?

1. _____

2. _____

3. _____

4. _____

5. _____

6. _____

7. _____

8. _____

9. _____

10. _____

These sound so cool! You should definitely do them – all of them!

My dad's brilliant at making stuff. That's *his* hobby. He made me my go-kart. It's really fast! And he's always doing do-it-yourself bits at home. Like putting up shelves... My dad puts up a lot of shelves!

Our hero number 7 wasn't known for being especially brilliant at making things. But what he wanted more than anything else was to make one particular thing.

Actually, to *re*-make it.

He couldn't do it on his own. He was going to need lots of people to help him.

But he knew it had to be done for God and for God's people. Even when God's enemies laughed at him and tried to stop his work, he kept going.

This hero's name was Nehemiah – and you're about to read the story of how **HE BECAME A SUPER-BUILDER** for God.

Nehemiah worked for the emperor of Persia. Persia was a long way from Jerusalem, but Jerusalem was the city Nehemiah's ancestors came from. It was where God's special people, the Israelites, used to live.

But there had been a war, and a lot of the city had been destroyed. There used to be a huge wall surrounding it to keep the Israelites' enemies out, but now the wall was smashed and broken.

Some of the Israelites were living in Jerusalem again, but they would never be safe.

The ruins also meant that God's enemies could have a good snigger at God and His people: 'Look at the state of God's city! He's obviously not powerful enough to clean it up, and His people don't seem to care…'

But one man did care: Nehemiah.

Far away in Persia, Nehemiah heard that Jerusalem was still in ruins and he was very sad. All he wanted was to see it re-made. Rebuilt. A place where God's people could live safely again. A place that would bring honour to God.

What do you think Nehemiah did? Crack the code and write down the words to find out.

⊠▽▷▽△□·▷ ▷◁·⊞▽⋗

_____

_____

Answer on page 110.

But Nehemiah couldn't just pack up and go to Jerusalem. He had an important job, working for the emperor, and would need his permission. But the emperor didn't know God, and probably didn't care about Jerusalem. So why would he let Nehemiah go?

He probably wouldn't – the only way for Nehemiah to get to Jerusalem and see how to rebuild it would be with God's help. Now, when God has a plan, things happen! And Nehemiah knew God had heard his prayers because, not just one, not even two – but FIVE things happened.

1. The emperor noticed Nehemiah was looking sad and asked him what was wrong.

2. Nehemiah was able to tell the emperor about Jerusalem.

3. When Nehemiah asked to go to Jerusalem to rebuild it, the emperor said, 'Yes!'.

4. The emperor gave Nehemiah all the wood he would need for the work from his own forests.

5. The emperor sent soldiers with Nehemiah to keep him safe on his journey.

You see? When God's on your side, **THINGS DEFINITELY HAPPEN!** It was time for Nehemiah to go travelling…

Can you help Nehemiah and the soldiers get to Jerusalem?

Answer on page 110.

When Nehemiah arrived, he didn't do anything straightaway. He didn't even tell anyone what his plans were.

Then, after three days, he went off on a donkey in the middle of the night to ride around the city. He looked at all the damage so he'd know what work had to be done.

What Nehemiah really needed now was a massive team of people to work together to help do the rebuilding.

They would have to pull together and work really hard. And the other thing they needed? A really good leader.

The Israelites who lived in broken Jerusalem didn't know where to start. They just didn't seem able to put everything back together. That's why God sent them a leader who could encourage them to pull together as a team. So God sent them His hero man, Nehemiah.

Nehemiah had enough hero power inside him to make God's people listen. When he told them what God had already done to help him, **THEY COULDN'T WAIT TO GET STARTED!**

It was hard work too. Nehemiah's team was made up of ordinary people who didn't know how to build! But Nehemiah made sure they knew God was right there with them, showing them what to do.

God's enemies didn't want Jerusalem to be put back together. They didn't want God's people to be safe. They didn't want His city to show His power again.

Nehemiah had just one answer for them.

Put the bricks in the right number order and write out the words to see what it was.

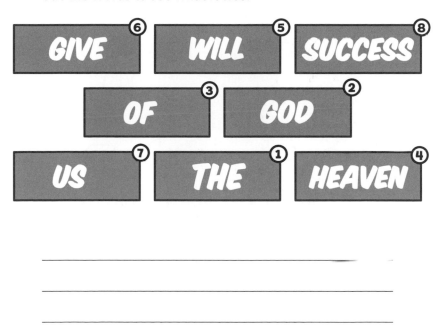

Wherever God sees a problem, He sees a way to fix it.

When we're sad, or lonely, or we're not sure what to do, God sees how to fix that too. He wants us to turn to Him and to talk to Him – to know that He is a loving friend who will never leave us.

Nehemiah couldn't bear to leave the city the way it was. It made him too sad. He had to do something and he needed God's help to do it.

That's why **NEHEMIAH** is our **HERO NUMBER 7!**

Is there anything in your life that needs mending? Maybe you feel sad about something. Maybe someone has been unkind to you and it's time to forgive them. Or maybe you just need to spend more time with God. Talk to Him now.

> God, thank You for Nehemiah. He rebuilt Jerusalem and made it strong again. All because he loved You. Please help me to be a builder, like him. Help me to trust that You will never leave me. I want to build my life on You. Amen.

8 DANIEL
Forever faithful
Read all about him in DANIEL 1 & 6

When I really want something, I don't give up easily. I won't let it go! Once I really wanted this amazing skateboard for my birthday, so I kept dropping hints: 'Dad, I think my old skateboard's starting to look a bit rough, don't you...?'

Our hero number 8, Daniel, wanted something. He wanted God. He wanted to hold on to God and keep Him in his life SO badly, nothing would make him let go.

There are lots of times in the Bible when, after a war, many of God's people were taken away from their homes to live in another country. They had to work as slaves there. That's what had happened to Daniel. He and lots of others were taken from their homeland in Judah to a country called Babylon.

But the people in Babylon didn't worship the Lord God. Instead, they worshipped gods that weren't real. And they lived in a different way from the way God's people lived.

It would have been easy for Daniel to just go along with the Babylon crowd and learn to fit in. But that's not what he did. God was too important to Daniel.

There's a big word that describes Daniel perfectly. Cross out every c, l, m and v, then write out the letters that are left to read what it is.

cvlSmtvvcemlalcvdmc
fclvmalclsvctmcl

_____

Answer on page 111.

While he was in Babylon, Daniel worked for the king. The king wanted Daniel to be strong and healthy. So, he ordered that he should be given the same food as was served at the royal table.

But Daniel didn't want to eat the king's food.

He wasn't being picky or ungrateful. It's just that God had told Daniel which foods he could eat and Daniel wanted to obey Him.

So Daniel stood up for God. **HE ASKED FOR JUST VEGETABLES INSTEAD.** Plain and simple!

The king's right-hand man was called Ashpenaz and he didn't like the idea. If Daniel ended up looking all thin and wishy-washy because he wasn't eating the king's food, Ashpenaz knew he'd be in big trouble.

But he needn't have worried. After ten days, Daniel looked way fitter and healthier than people who *were* eating the king's food.

Daniel wasn't surprised. He knew that if he kept God at the number 1 spot in his life, God would be with him to help him every step of the way.

But doing what God wants isn't always easy. No matter how much Daniel wanted to obey God, I bet the king's food looked really scrummy. It might have been quite hard to turn down. But even if Daniel was tempted to eat it, he didn't. **HE PUT GOD FIRST. ALWAYS.**

Crack the code and write out the words to discover something really helpful the Bible teaches about temptation.

⊙∀⋗ '⯐⯐⊟⊟ ⊠∀⊕ ∧⊟⊟∀⯐ ⊞∀⯐
⊕∀ ⯐∀ ⊕∀⊲⊙∀⋗ ⯐∀⊞∀⊠⋗
⊞∀⯐⊲ ⋗∀⯐∀⊲ ⊕∀ ⊲∀∧∧⯐⊠
⋗⯐⊲∧'

_____

_____

Answer in 1 Corinthians 10 v 13.

A	B	C	D	E	F	G	H	I	J	K	L	M
∧	◫	⊙	⋗	▽	⋌	⊳	⊙	▷	⯐	⊲	⊟	∧

N	O	P	Q	R	S	T	U	V	W	X	Y	Z
⊠	∀	▷	⊳	⊲	⊲	⊕	⊡	⊲	⯐	⊖	⊞	⊲

When it comes to 'remaining firm', Daniel was a winner – on top of the podium, waving a trophy.

And God wants us to be winners like Daniel. So you can be absolutely sure that He'll be right beside you, cheering you on, when you ask for His help!

But there was another time when Daniel showed even more superhero staying-power. It was when there was a new king of Babylon.

King Darius saw what a good worker Daniel was, so he promoted him. He wanted Daniel to be in charge of his whole kingdom. This should have been stonking news for Daniel… but it didn't turn out that way.

Some other men who worked for the king were jealous. They made a plan to trap Daniel. They advised the king to make an order: for the next 30 days, people weren't allowed to pray to any god – only to the king. And if anyone got caught breaking the order? Well, they'd be thrown into the lion pit – where there were some very hungry lions. Nasty!

So, what do you think Daniel did? Did he…

1. Only talk to God when he really needed something - and very, very quietly?
YES ☐ NO ☐

2. Only talk to God when he was sure no one would see him?
YES ☐ NO ☐

3. Tell God he'd talk to Him again in 30 days' time?
YES ☐ NO ☐

4. Carry on talking to God the way he'd always done - three times a day, sitting by his window?
YES ☐ NO ☐

Answers on page 111.

It takes a MEGA amount of staying-power to do what Daniel did. If he was caught praying to God, he knew he'd be munched on by a bunch of scary lions! But that didn't stop him. **GOD WAS THE MOST IMPORTANT THING IN DANIEL'S LIFE,** and he would never let Him go. And the jealous men saw to it that Daniel ended up in the lion pit because of it.

But God saw to it that Daniel didn't end up with a single tooth mark on his body! He sent an angel into the lion pit to keep the lions' mouths shut tight. Phew!

King Darius could hardly believe it. He was also over the moon, because he actually really liked Daniel. It's just that he'd been tricked into making a law that he couldn't break.

Use the lions' teeth to fill in the missing word...

The king could now see that Daniel was 100% ____ ____ ____ ____ ____ to God.

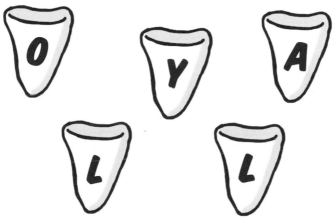

Answer on page 111.

But it wasn't just Daniel who the king thought was awesome. It was God too!

King Darius had the jealous men rounded up. And the lions – still hungry having missed out on their dinner – had some breakfast instead...

Did you know that there are loads of types of big cats in the world – all with very sharp teeth? They live out in the wild in lots of different countries.

Here's a list of 10 big cats. Maybe you could look them up online to see what they all look like! Try to find them in the word search.

CHEETAH
LEOPARD
COUGAR
JAGUAR
LION
TIGER
LYNX
PUMA
WILD CAT
OCELOT

W	E	R	W	I	N	C	B	R	W	C	V
S	A	I	E	N	O	C	V	L	H	O	V
T	X	B	Z	G	M	B	F	E	H	U	R
C	N	E	C	M	I	Y	E	G	K	G	X
F	Y	D	B	N	S	T	B	I	W	A	A
T	L	E	O	P	A	R	D	N	T	R	U
A	N	M	N	H	B	P	L	O	I	A	M
C	G	O	K	E	U	V	P	U	M	A	K
D	I	L	R	N	T	Z	R	R	S	S	N
L	H	R	A	U	G	A	J	T	B	J	O
I	Y	K	M	O	S	W	E	A	B	Z	P
W	I	J	Q	P	R	O	C	E	L	O	T

Answer on page 111.

God is totally faithful to us. When we want to talk to Him, He is always there to listen. When we need His help, **HE WILL NEVER LET US DOWN.**

God wants us to be faithful to Him too. But if we mess up and make mistakes, He doesn't stomp off in a huff, muttering, 'Well, that's the last time I help *you* out!'

He stays patient and loving.

When God's Son, Jesus, lived with people on the earth, He felt everything we feel. Jesus felt:

- **Hungry**
- **Thirsty**
- **Happy**
- **Excited**
- **Sad**
- **Cold**
- **Hot**
- **Tired**
- **Even angry sometimes!**

Jesus knew exactly what it was like to be a human being. And that means He was tempted to do things God wouldn't like, just the way we are. He never gave in to temptation – not once – but He still knew what it was like to have those feelings. Because Jesus knows what it's like, God knows too. That's why God always understands and is ready to step in when we ask Him to.

God protected Daniel when Daniel needed Him most. Daniel had superhero staying-power and loyalty and, wow, didn't God reward him for it!

Something else fantastic came out of Daniel's loyalty to God. King Darius wanted to know God too – and he commanded everyone living in his whole empire to get to know Him!

Follow the read-around to see what the king said…

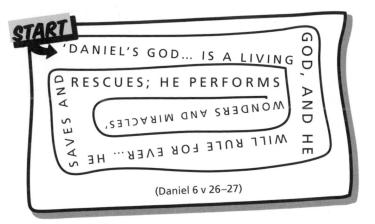

START

'DANIEL'S GOD… IS A LIVING GOD, AND HE WILL RULE FOR EVER… HE SAVES AND RESCUES; HE PERFORMS WONDERS AND MIRACLES.'

(Daniel 6 v 26–27)

Daniel's loyalty made a loyal follower out of King Darius. What a stonking hero for God! That's **DANIEL,** our **HERO NUMBER 8.** Pray this prayer now!

God, the story of Daniel is amazing! It shows me what it truly means to be a superhero for You! Nothing in a king's whole kingdom would make Daniel let go of You. Let nothing ever take me away from loving and serving You with my whole heart. Amen.

9 ESTHER
For a time like this

Read all about her in the book of **ESTHER**

All the heroes in this book were super-keen on God and living for Him. **GOD MEANT EVERYTHING TO THEM.**

That's not to say that they didn't think for themselves. Or that they all worked for God in exactly the same way. Or that they never made a single mistake (some of them made big mistakes before they actually got to know God).

But God was HUGE in their lives. And when God is that important to people, He knows He can give them a nudge and say: 'Hey! I'd like you to do something for me…'

> But working for God doesn't have to mean anything fancy. Just doing simple, everyday things – keeping God right in the centre of all of them – makes Him very happy.

Cross out every x, b, j and z to read something Jesus once said – and then actually did.

'bbjThexbxgreatestjjbzlovezbjyouzx
zcanbjbbhavezxforzbyourjbxxfriendsz
zisbjjtoxbjgivejzbyourzxxjlifejbjforzxj
bthem.'

_____

_____

_____

_____

Answer in John 15 v 13.

Hero number 9 in our Topz 10 lived up to those words too, but way, *way* before they were even spoken.

Esther has to be one of the coolest queens ever! And she wasn't even born to be a queen. In fact, it probably never crossed her mind that she might one day be someone so important.

But here's what made Esther such a superhero – she was… (Trace over the words!)

OPEN TO
GOD'S PLANS

Esther was a young girl who lived in a country called Persia. Both her parents had died, so her cousin, Mordecai, looked after her. But Esther and Mordecai weren't Persian. They were Jews (Israelites). The Jews were a special people to God and lots of them had been taken to Persia as prisoners during a war (much like Daniel, our hero number 8!).

One day, Xerxes (you say it like 'Zerk-sees'), the king of Persia, held a huge party. Lots of important people came and the king was very happy because he could do a lot of showing off. But King Xerxes made a BIG mistake. One of the things he wanted to show off was his wife, Queen Vashti, because she was so beautiful. Bad idea…

When the king ordered Queen Vashti to join the party, what do you think she said? Tick your answer.

'I won't be long, I'm just washing my hair.' ☐

'Ooh, I love a party – I'll be right there!' ☐

'Can I bring a friend?' ☐

'NO!' ☐

Queen Vashti didn't want to be 'shown off'. After all, she was a person, not a 'thing'. So, if you ticked 'NO', you're righter than right! And guess how King Xerxes felt – madder than mad!

In fact, the king was SO mad that he sent Queen Vashti away. (Bit silly, really, because there Xerxes was, suddenly wifeless and queenless.)

Draw what the king's face must have looked like.

So – the search was on for a new wife and queen.

And that's how it was that Esther became the brand-new queen of Persia! Of all the young women from his kingdom that King Xerxes met, Esther was the one he chose to be his wife.

But Mordecai told Esther not to tell the king she was a Jew. Sometimes people don't like others who are different from them. So no one at the palace knew.

There was a man called Haman who worked for the king. He was quite powerful and the king liked him a lot.

But Haman didn't like Jewish people. He especially didn't like Mordecai.

You see, Mordecai worshipped God. He worshipped *only* God. And when Haman ordered everyone to bow down and worship *him*, Mordecai refused.

So Haman hated him. He hated Mordecai so much that he went to the king. He told Xerxes that the Jews weren't like the Persian people. They did things the Persians didn't do, and they didn't do things the Persian people did do.

Then he asked the king to order that all the Jews in the kingdom should be killed! What do you think the king said? Tick your answer.

1. 'That sounds a bit extreme.' ☐

2. 'I'm just off for a bath, I'll think about it later.' ☐

3. 'Oh, not another order! I hate being king!' ☐

4. 'YES!' ☐

Did you tick number **4**? Because that's what the king said: 'YES!' And he stamped the royal order using the special ring that he wore.

But, of course, what King Xerxes didn't know was that Esther – his own wife, the queen – was a Jew.

And the king wasn't the only one. Haman didn't know either.

The Jewish people needed a hero… and it was time for Esther to step up to the mark! Not Esther, the young girl. Not even Esther, the queen of Persia.

No! What the Jewish people needed now was Esther, *THE SUPERHERO!*

Now Esther didn't actually have to do a thing. After all, no one knew she was Jewish. If she just kept quiet, she'd be safe – wouldn't she?

But that wasn't good enough. Not for Esther. How could she stand by and see all her people killed? She couldn't! She knew she had to do something to stop this terrible order. She had to speak with the king. The trouble was, that wasn't as easy as it sounds…

No one was allowed to go and see the king unless he asked for them. Not even his wife. If anyone did, the king could have them put to death! It was the law.

But what else could Esther do? However scary going to the king would be, she was the only one who might be able to rescue the Jews. And these were God's own special people. So wouldn't God help her?

Mordecai believed that God would. Follow the read-around to see what Mordecai said to Esther.

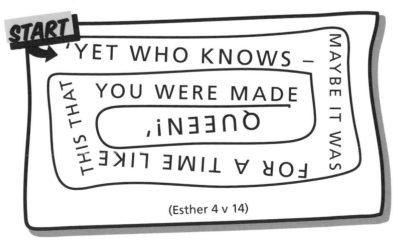

START

'YET WHO KNOWS – MAYBE IT WAS FOR A TIME LIKE THIS THAT YOU WERE MADE QUEEN!'

(Esther 4 v 14)

Did you know that God can't wait to hear from you? He wants you to talk to Him about everything. He wants to hear about your day – the things you've done, the people you've chatted to, what you've learnt.

GOD REALLY IS A BEST FRIEND WHO WANTS TO BE A PART OF EVERYTHING IN YOUR LIFE.

So, when something's wrong and there are problems, He's first in line calling out: 'Talk to me, talk to me!'

Esther knew that.

This was the biggest and scariest thing she had ever had to do. So talking to God was top of her list!

And she didn't talk to Him on her own either. She asked Mordecai to get all the Jews in the city together so that they could pray too. And Esther prayed in the palace with her servants.

As well as that, they all fasted. They didn't eat or drink a thing for three days and nights to show God how serious they were in their prayers.

Esther wasn't going to rush into anything – not without having God right there with her.

No food or drink for three days and nights? Wow! That is serious!

What's important to us is important to God!

Is there anything in your head right now that really matters to you? Are you worried about something? Is there something you'd like God to do for you or for someone else?

Whatever it is you want to say to God, He is always waiting to hear from you. Why not use this space to write a prayer to Him? You can either talk to Him about help you need, like Esther. Or, if everything is going great at the moment, why not write a prayer of praise instead?

_____

_____

_____

_____

_____

_____

_____

_____

God never left Esther. Not for one single, tiny second. When Esther went to talk to the king, he was pleased to see her – so he didn't have her killed!

But that's not the only miracle that happened. When Esther explained that she was one of the Jews Haman wanted killed, the king took her side – and it was Haman who was put to death! The Jews were saved!

Esther helped save her people because she had hero selflessness. That means she cared a million times more about others than she did about herself.

SHE WAS AFRAID, BUT SHE TRUSTED GOD.

She was open to Him and what He wanted her to do. After all, God had made her queen 'for a time like this' – hadn't He?

So that's our **HERO NUMBER 9, ESTHER!** Why not pray this prayer now?

> *God, thank You for always being with me. Please use me in Your plans. I want to be open to You every day – ready to be where You want me to be and to do what You want me to do. Amen.*

10 PAUL
A brand-new man
Read all about him in **ACTS 9**

My name's Benny. It's always been Benny.

Sometimes, Mum calls me Benjamin (often when I'm in trouble!). But usually, I'm just Benny. Because that's my name and I can't see it ever changing.

But some people use different names – like actors and authors. That might be because there's already an actor or author with their name, so they need to find something different.

When people get married, the bride usually drops her own surname (her 'maiden' name) and takes her husband's surname instead. And, in some cultures, people might change their name if some other significant thing happens in their life.

That's a bit like our hero number 10. His name was Saul. But he had another name too – Paul.

Do you have a middle name? Write it here.

_____

Do you have a nickname? Write it here.

_____

Saul was from a Hebrew (Israelite) family, and Saul was his Hebrew name. The Bible says that he was 'also known as Paul' (Acts 13 v 9). Paul was a Roman name, and when Saul began teaching people who weren't Israelites about Jesus, Paul is the name that he came to be known by.

Just so it's not too confusing, we're going to call him Paul from now on. That's the name that's mostly used in the New Testament.

What can I say? It's a great name!

Paul started out as one of the most unlikely people in the whole world ever to be a hero for God. Not because he was ordinary or nervous or his faith wasn't up to much.

PAUL DIDN'T SEEM LIKE HERO MATERIAL

because he hated Jesus and His followers.

You see, Paul was a Pharisee (one of the religious leaders who hated Jesus' teaching because it went against their ideas of what faith in God should look like).

Paul doesn't appear in the Bible until after Jesus has died and gone back to heaven. But before Jesus went, He told His friends, the disciples, to do something very important (write the words the right way round to discover what).

'oG tuohguorht eht elohw dlrow dna hcaerp eht lepsog ot lla elpoep.'

_____

_____

_____

Answer in Mark 16 v 15.

The book of Acts in the New Testament is all about the disciples and other believers doing exactly what Jesus had asked them to do. And Paul hated them for it.

Paul hated them so much that he had lots of them thrown into prison!

Paul wanted to stop the news of Jesus spreading. So he tried to get rid of all the Christians. He even let a man called Stephen be killed for what he taught and believed (remember hero number 4?).

Well – how likely was it that God would choose a man like that to be a hero for Him?

Very likely, as it turned out!

Paul headed off for a city called Damascus. He planned to hunt out all the believers there and put them in prison. But it never happened. **ON THE JOURNEY, JESUS TURNED UP!** Not in an actual face-to-face type way, but in a dazzling light. Paul was terrified, shut his eyes tight and fell down onto the ground!

From out of the light, Jesus asked Paul why he was picking on Him and His followers so much. Then He gave instructions to Paul to carry on to Damascus where he must wait to be told what to do.

But when he opened his eyes, he couldn't see a thing. **HE WAS BLIND!**

Pretend for a minute that you're a journalist (a newspaper reporter). You've been sent to find out exactly what's gone on along the road to Damascus. Then you have to write up an exciting report about it.

But what you really need is a super-catchy, front-page headline – the title for the story – so that people will grab a copy of your newspaper.

See what you can come up with! When you've thought of something snappy, write it on the newspaper below.

Because Paul couldn't see, he had to be led to Damascus by someone holding his hand. When he got there, he must have still been really jittery. He didn't eat or drink anything for three days.

But God was on the case. He spoke to a man called Ananias.

'Go and see Paul,' God said. 'Make his eyes better and I will fill him with my Spirit.'

God sent His Holy Spirit to live inside people to help them live His way, and to make them brave enough to tell other people about Him. God's Spirit was going to do something totally amazing in Paul!

Ananias didn't want to go to visit Paul. He was probably a bit scared – he'd heard all about this man and how cruel he was to people who believed in Jesus. But God wasn't taking no for an answer. Follow the arrows to read what He said to Ananias about Paul.

'because Go, have I him chosen serve to me'

_____

_____

Answer in Acts 9 v 15.

Wow! Imagine our awesome, holy, perfect God choosing someone as mean and nasty as Paul to work for Him! But God isn't like us. God is unbelievably forgiving. He sees what we are, but much more than that – **HE SEES WHAT WE CAN BE!**

God saw what a hard-worker Paul could be for Him if he'd just let go of his hate, and invite the Holy Spirit in. But it would be an E-N-O-R-M-O-U-S change in Paul's life!

Sometimes change can be exciting – sometimes it can seem scary.

What changes have you gone through? Have you moved house or school? Have you become a big brother or sister?

Write down anything you can think of that has changed in your life. Then write next to it what the change was like for you – 'exciting' or 'scary'.

_____ _____

_____ _____

_____ _____

_____ _____

_____ _____

_____ _____

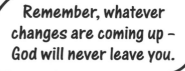

Remember, whatever changes are coming up – God will never leave you.

God changed Paul into a completely different person. If it wasn't for the fact that he still *looked* the same, no one would have recognised him!

A
ANGRY
CRUEL
VENGEFUL
NASTY
HATEFUL
RUTHLESS

B
PRAYERFUL
HUMBLE
LOVING
DEDICATED
OBEDIENT
HARD-WORKING

The Holy Spirit changed him from being all the things under A, into being all the things under B.

That's a MASSIVE change!

Can you find all those words in the word search?

V	D	J	W	O	P	R	A	Y	E	R	F	U	L
Q	E	J	D	C	L	T	E	R	S	K	L	X	P
R	D	N	P	I	R	L	N	F	E	J	O	C	I
H	I	B	G	N	V	U	W	E	F	H	R	V	G
N	C	H	D	E	A	X	T	G	I	G	F	B	N
S	A	X	C	H	F	N	E	H	G	D	M	N	I
T	T	S	R	Y	H	U	M	B	L	E	E	M	K
U	E	C	T	B	A	W	L	A	B	E	T	B	R
B	D	O	A	Y	S	O	D	S	H	M	S	D	O
T	R	L	B	G	V	A	I	W	B	M	A	S	W
E	E	D	L	I	V	F	C	R	U	E	L	M	D
N	D	P	N	T	F	C	A	J	G	L	N	G	R
A	N	G	R	Y	R	N	S	D	E	M	U	B	A
R	T	Y	U	I	O	P	L	U	F	E	T	A	H

Paul had hero willingness to let God turn his life inside out and back to front for Him. To let God make him completely new! **AND THAT'S WHEN PAUL'S ADVENTURES BEGAN.**

He visited lots of cities in different countries. Everywhere he went, he taught people who Jesus was and about what He had done. And he set up churches too!

Paul had been changed by God. So he went out and changed other people by introducing them to Jesus.

Paul's life wasn't easy. There were people who hated him for teaching about Jesus, just as he used to hate Christians too. He was thrown in prison; he was attacked. There were even people trying to kill him.

But nothing stopped hero Paul. He helped Christians, even when he wasn't with them. A lot of the letters you can find in the New Testament were written by Paul to different churches.

He wrote four helpful letters from inside prison too! Unscramble the letters below to see who Paul wrote to while he was locked up.

1. **pehnsEias** _____

2. **hpiaplisPin** _____

3. **lCnoiosass** _____

4. **Pnhiemlo** _____

Answers on page 111.

Some of the most famous words Paul wrote in a letter are about love. They go like this…

'Love is patient and kind; it is not jealous or conceited or proud; love is not ill-mannered or selfish or irritable; love does not keep a record of wrongs; love is not happy with evil, but is happy with the truth. Love never gives up; and its faith, hope, and patience never fail. Love is eternal.' (1 Corinthians 13 v 4–8)

Can you believe it? Paul, who used to be so full of hate, wrote something like that about love!

Even though Paul had hurt God so much, God stepped into Paul's life and gave him a chance to live it in a totally different way. A hero's way. And that's why **PAUL** is our **HERO NUMBER 10!**

Whatever wrong things we've done, God can make us all brand new. We just have to let Him. Why not pray this prayer now?

God, I praise You for being so kind and so forgiving. Thank You for being everything that love is. Paul shows me how You find the hero inside people. Please find the hero inside me, God, so that I can live for You. Amen.

THERE ARE HEROES OUTSIDE THE BIBLE TOO!

All Benny and Paul's Topz 10 heroes are from the Bible. But God didn't stop there. He's at work in people all the time – right now, this second, as well as way back in the past.

So here's a quick look at two much more modern-day heroes...

ERIC LIDDELL

Eric Liddell was Scottish, but he was born in China in 1902. His parents both worked there as missionaries.

Eric became so good at running that, in 1924, he competed in the Paris Olympics.

He was going to run in the 100-metre sprint, the race he was best at. But then Eric found out that the race itself would be held on a Sunday.

Eric's whole life was built on God. And the Bible said that Sunday was God's day. For Eric, that meant it wouldn't be right to race on that day.

Although he might lose his chance to win a medal, he pulled out of the 100-metre sprint and entered the 400-metre race instead. Eric wasn't usually as good at running longer distances, but that didn't matter. The important thing was that those races weren't to be held on a Sunday.

WHAT AN INCREDIBLE WAY TO PUT GOD FIRST! Eric showed hero commitment and respect towards his Father God.

Because of that, God honoured him. Eric still won a gold medal – for the 400-metre race. And he won a bronze medal for the 200-metre race too!

NICKY CRUZ

Nicky Cruz was born in 1938 in Puerto Rico. His family life was very unhappy and, when he was 15, he went to live with his brother in New York. There, he joined a street gang, and soon became their leader.

Now, street gangs are nothing like Topz. And Nicky Cruz's gang did a lot of very bad and horrible things. Some of the gang members even ended up in prison for the things they did.

One day, Nicky heard a man telling people how much God loved them. Nicky didn't believe that anyone loved him. Then soon afterwards, he went along to a church meeting – not to listen, but to cause trouble.

AND THAT'S WHERE HE HEARD ABOUT JESUS!

Nicky asked God to forgive him for all the things he'd done, and from that moment his whole life changed. He left the gang, went to Bible College, and began to teach young people from street gangs that God loved them. Through his teaching, lots of young people just like him were saved because they got to know God too.

God sees the hero inside ordinary, everyday people, like you and like me. It's up to us to learn to trust Him to use His power inside us to set that hero free! So, what do you think? Are you up for it?

ANSWERS

Page 20
Shem, Ham, Japheth

Page 22

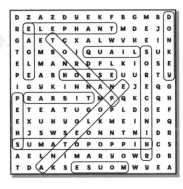

Page 29
Love
Joy
Peace
Patience
Kindness
Goodness
Faithfulness
Humility
Self-control

Page 61
1. False
2. False
3. False
4. True
5. True
6. False
7. True

Page 63
hiding place

Page 71
Nehemiah prayed

Page 73

Page 78
Steadfast

Page 81
1. No
2. No
3. No
4. Yes

Page 83
Loyal

Page 84

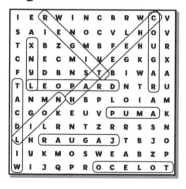

Page 104

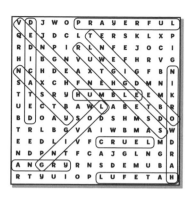

Page 105
1. Ephesians
2. Philippians
3. Colossians
4. Philemon

To check answers found in the Bible, you will need a Good News Bible. This version is available online.

TOPZ EVERY DAY

Topz is an exciting, day-by-day look at the Bible with the Topz Gang! Full of fun activities, cartoons, prayers and daily Bible readings – dive in and get to know God and His Word!

Available as an annual subscription or as single issues. Find out more at **www.cwr.org.uk/topzeveryday**

MORE TOPZ

There are four different series of *Topz* books for you to discover! Find out more at **www.cwr.org.uk/topzbooks**